LEADING WOMEN

Barbara Jordan

LUCIA RAATMA

Cavendish
Square

New York

Published in 2014 by Cavendish Square Publishing, LLC
303 Park Avenue South, Suite 1247, New York, NY 10010

First Edition

Website: cavendishsq.com

CPSIA Compliance Information: Batch #WS13CSQ

All websites were available and accurate when this book was sent to press.

Library of Congress Cataloging-in-Publication Data
Raatma, Lucia.
Barbara Jordan / Lucia Raatma.
p. cm. — (Leading women)
Includes bibliographical references and index.
Summary: "Presents the biography of Barbara Jordan against the backdrop of
her political, historical, and cultural environment"—Provided by publisher.
ISBN 978-0-7614-4956-0 (hardcover) — ISBN 978-1-62712-114-9 (paperback)
— ISBN 978-1-60870-713-3 (ebook)
1. Jordan, Barbara, 1936-1996—Juvenile literature. 2. Legislators—United States—Biography—Juvenile literature. 3. African American women legislators—United States—Biography—Juvenile literature. 4. United States. Congress. House—Biography—Juvenile literature. 5. African American women legislators—Texas—Biography—Juvenile literature. 6. Texas—Politics and government—1951—Juvenile literature. I. Title.
E840.8.J62R33 2012
328.73'092—dc22 [B]
2011003470

Editor: Deborah Grahame-Smith   Series Designer: Nancy Sabato   Art Director: Anahid Hamparian
Photo research by Connie Gardner

Cover photo by State Preservation Board, Austin, Texas; Accession ID CHA 1989.368. Photographer Eric Beggs 7/14/1995 Post Conservation.

The photographs in this book are used by permission and through the courtesy of: AP Photo; 4, 28, 32, 43, 65, 72, 80; Barbara Jordan Archives: 6, 15, 18, 20, 44, 60; Getty Images; Buyenlarge/Contributor, 10; Anthony Potter Collection, 11; Bachrach, 26; Time and Life, 58; David Hume Kennerly, 67; Corbis: Hulton Deutsch, 13; Bettmann, 36, 51; Corbis, 40; The Image Works; Topham, 30; Bob Daemmrich 84.

Printed in the United States of America

CONTENTS

Barbara Jordan greets the audience before giving the keynote speech at the Democratic National Convention on July 12, 1976.

The Keynote Speech

In summer 1976 in New York City, the Democratic Party held its convention to nominate its official candidate for president of the United States. Then, as now, two political parties dominated the nation: the Democrats and the Republicans. This was a big year for the Democrats, who hoped to win the election after two terms of Republican presidents. But this was not the only reason that the convention was important. It marked the first time that an African-American woman delivered a keynote speech at a major political party's convention. That woman was Barbara Jordan.

While addressing the convention, Jordan reminded the delegates of the Democratic Party's history:

"First, we believe in equality for all and privileges for none. This is a belief—this is a belief that each American, regardless of background, has equal standing in the public forum—all of us. Because we believe this idea so firmly, we are an inclusive rather than an exclusive party. Let everybody come. . . .

We believe that the government which represents the authority of all people, not just one interest group, but all the people, has an obligation to actively underscore, actively seek to remove those obstacles which would block individual achievement, obstacles emanating from race, sex, economic condition. The government must seek to remove them. . . .

We are a party of innovation. We do not reject our traditions, but we are willing to adapt to changing circumstances, when change we must. We are willing to suffer the discomfort of change in order to achieve a better future."

Jordan grabbed the nation's attention and proved to be a compelling and influential speaker. According to a list compiled by researchers, her address at the Democratic National Convention ranks as the fifth most influential speech of the twentieth century in the United States.

CHAPTER ONE

Early Life

BARBARA CHARLINE JORDAN WAS BORN ON February 21, 1936, in Houston, Texas. The United States was in the midst of the Great Depression, a time marked by widespread unemployment and a poor economy. Her parents, Arlyne and Benjamin Jordan, had two other daughters, Bennie and Rose Mary. Benjamin's parents, Alice and Charles Jordan, lived with the family in a red brick home in Houston's Fifth Ward, a neighborhood created shortly after the Civil War (1861–1865). In the 1930s, the Fifth Ward was populated primarily by African American working-class people.

Barbara's other grandfather, John Ed Patten, owned a junkyard. At one time he had been very successful, but a series of racially motivated incidents had changed the course of his life. He had become angry and withdrawn. He wasn't fond of his son-in-law, nor was he close to his daughter, Arlyne. But when Barbara was born, something shifted. He formed an immediate attachment to this granddaughter.

While growing up, Barbara developed a special bond with Grandpa Patten and helped him in the junkyard. He called her his business partner. Grandpa Patten always listened to Barbara. He had a feeling that she was destined to accomplish great things. He once told her,

" Don't ever marry, and don't work for anybody except yourself. "

Young Barbara poses with her two sisters, Bennie and Rose Mary, in Houston.

THE GREAT DEPRESSION

The Great Depression was the worst economic downturn in modern history. Many experts consider October 29, 1929—the day the U.S. stock market crashed—as the period's starting point. The Great Depression, which was marked by mass unemployment and decreased industry, affected countries all over the world. Banks closed, farms failed, and many people lost their homes. To inject life back into the economy, President Franklin D. Roosevelt created the New Deal. This was a work program that gave people jobs building schools, roads, bridges, state parks, and other public works. In the United States, the Great Depression began to ease during World War II (1939–1945), when U.S. industries increased production on military supplies.

Throughout her life, Barbara carried photos of Patten with her.

Benjamin Jordan worked hard in his job at the Houston Terminal Warehouse and Cold Storage. He expected his daughters to be proper and well behaved. He didn't tolerate poor schoolwork or laziness. Sometimes ruling the house with an iron fist, he prohibited the girls from attending movies or dances. He balanced strictness with devotion, however. Benjamin often attended school programs and helped the girls with homework. He once told Barbara,

 I'll stick with you as far as you want to go.

She knew he was encouraging her to figure out what she wanted to do with her life and not to let anything slow her down.

GOOD HOPE BAPTIST CHURCH

Young Barbara attended services at Good Hope Baptist Church with her family. Her father was a deacon for the church. For the Jordans and many other African-American families, churches were very important gathering places. Within the walls of their churches, African Americans were free to talk about their feelings of inequality, and they were encouraged to fight the injustices around them. The minister at Good Hope Baptist, Reverend Alfred A. Lucas, was a political activist. In addition to leading the church, he helped organize the Houston branch of the National Association for the Advancement of Colored People (NAACP).

At this time in U.S. history, African Americans faced inequality and segregation. They were not allowed in many public places, such

Members of an African-American church gather on Sunday morning.

as certain hotels and restaurants, and they went to all-black schools. Sometimes they had to use separate sections in movie theaters and waiting rooms, and they even had to drink from water fountains different from those designated for white people. Sometimes light-skinned African Americans tried to "pass" as white so that they would not be mistreated.

The NAACP fought to protect the rights of African Americans, and Reverend Lucas often spoke of these issues during his sermons at Good Hope Baptist. He also held NAACP meetings at the church, so Barbara was exposed to politics at a very young age.

THE BEGINNING OF THE NAACP

The National Association for the Advancement of Colored People is a nonprofit interracial organization that was founded in 1909. Its mission is "to ensure the political, educational, social, and economic equality of rights of all persons and to eliminate racial hatred and racial discrimination." In the early 1900s, when black Americans were experiencing all types of prejudice, including unfair voter registration practices, a group of people decided to create the NAACP as a way to fight the injustices. Among the founders were poet and activist W. E. B. Du Bois, lawyer Archibald Grimké, and women's suffrage leader Mary White Ovington. While *colored people* is an outdated term for African Americans, it remains in the organization's name as part of its history. Today, the NAACP gives out Image Awards and Spingarn Medals to recognize excellence among black Americans.

Staff members work in an NAACP office in 1944.

When she was ten years old, Barbara decided to be baptized and officially joined the church. The Good Hope Baptist community was important to her and her family. Barbara held fast to her Christian beliefs throughout her entire life.

A NEW PART OF HOUSTON

A few years later, when Barbara was thirteen, her father decided to become a minister himself. The family had to leave the Fifth Ward and move to Houston Heights. This was a huge adjustment for Barbara. Benjamin had become the minister of Greater Pleasant Hill Baptist Church, which did not have the same sense of community that Good Hope had. Barbara missed her grandparents, her friends, and her old church.

The Jordans made the best of their move, however. While Rose Mary went off to college, Bennie and Barbara helped start a singing group. The group sang at churches throughout Houston, and Barbara recited poetry at the performances as well. Even at a young age, her voice was already strong and compelling.

IN HIGH SCHOOL

Before long, Barbara entered Phillis Wheatley High School, which was considered Houston's best school for African Americans. She enjoyed her classes and after-school activities. She had a good group of friends, sang in the girls' choir, and served as president of the honor society.

Barbara noticed discrimination within her school, however. She found that the most popular girls were light skinned, and teachers seemed to play favorites with the light-skinned students. Some of the

A youth choir sings in church. Barbara Jordan honed her vocal skills in a choir like this one.

students resorted to using bleach to lighten their skin, but Barbara, whose skin was dark, never did that. She had been raised to be proud of her appearance and heritage. She once commented,

> **The world had decided we were all Negro, but that some of us were more Negro than others.**

While in high school, Barbara set an important goal: she wanted to be the best public speaker in school. Barbara immediately

PHILLIS WHEATLEY

Phillis Wheatley High School was named for a remarkable woman. Born in West Africa, the girl who became Phillis Wheatley (1753–1784) was kidnapped at age seven. She traveled to Boston on the slave ship *Phillis*, from which she got her first name. John Wheatley, a wealthy businessman, purchased her. Wheatley's wife and daughter took an interest in Phillis and taught her to read and write. She became the first published African-American poet and helped create the genre of African-American literature. Wheatley's book *Poems on Various Subjects, Religious and Moral*, which was published in 1773, gained her much fame. However, when she died at age thirty-one, she was living in poverty.

impressed Ashton Jerome, Phillis Wheatley's speech teacher, who asked her to join the school's speech team. Entering and winning contest after contest, she excelled on the team. After doing well at the local level, she moved on to the National United Ushers Association Oratorical Contest.

Barbara took her first trip out of Texas to attend the competition, which was held in Chicago. Barbara had memorized her speech and was confident as she approached

Barbara Jordan celebrates her high school graduation day in 1952.

the podium. Her skill and confidence shone brightly, and she won first place. Due to all of her accomplishments, Barbara was named Phillis Wheatley High School Girl of the Year before she graduated in 1952.

LOOKING TO THE FUTURE

Another important event took place when Barbara was in high school. A woman named Edith Sampson came to speak to the students, and Barbara's life was changed forever. Sampson was a successful lawyer with a degree from Loyola University in Chicago. In the school's audi-

EDITH SAMPSON

Edith Sampson (c. 1901–1979) was born in Pittsburgh, Pennsylvania. She went to school to become a social worker. One of her instructors encouraged her to become a lawyer, however, and she began taking evening classes at John Marshall Law School. She then enrolled in Loyola University Law School, and in 1927 she became the first woman to receive a master of law degree from Loyola. Sampson opened a law practice on Chicago's South Side and served the African-American community. Later, she served as assistant state's attorney for Cook County and became the first African-American delegate to the United Nations. In 1962, she became the first African-American woman in the United States to become a judge by popular vote. She served on Cook County's circuit court until she retired in 1978.

torium, she spoke to the students about her work and encouraged them to pursue careers in law.

Barbara was impressed. Sampson was well spoken and well dressed. She seemed so intelligent and sure of herself. Right then and there, Barbara knew she wanted to be a lawyer. Others wondered about such an idea. In the 1950s, people expected women to get married and to raise children. At that time, the idea of an African-American woman becoming a lawyer seemed rather far-fetched. Could Barbara really do it?

In the meantime, Barbara's father had taken a job back at Good Hope Baptist Church. Barbara and her family were thrilled to be going back to their old neighborhood. The future looked bright.

CHAPTER TWO

Becoming a Lawyer

A S BARBARA JORDAN CONSIDERED WHICH college to attend, she carefully weighed her options. Not all schools were open to African Americans in 1952. Because many public universities were still segregated, black Americans were not allowed.

Finally, Barbara decided on Texas Southern University (TSU) in Houston, where her sister Bennie had gone. The Texas legislature had established TSU to provide an option for African-American students, since they were often denied admission to other Texas colleges.

ON THE DEBATE TEAM

Once at college, Jordan made a point to seek out the debate coach, Tom Freeman. He had once been a judge at one of her high school speech contests. Though she hadn't won that contest, Freeman said he had voted for her to take first place. Jordan tried out for the debate team, as did Otis King, a classmate from Phillis Wheatley High School. Freeman accepted them both.

The TSU team won lots of tournaments. They debated other African-American students until TSU traveled to a tournament at Baylor University in Waco. This marked the first time that an African-American team faced a white debate team in the South. From there, TSU's team went on to debate students from the University of Chicago, Harvard University, and New York University. These experiences were of great value to Jordan. She

Barbara Jordan (*upper right*) attends a party with a group of friends in Houston.

Barbara Jordan participates in a competition with her TSU debate team.

learned to research and organize information, honed her speaking skills, and saw cities all over the country.

ON TO LAW SCHOOL

During her senior year, before graduating with honors in 1956, Jordan considered what she would do next. She knew she wanted to go to law school, but where? There were many fine schools to consider, but she had to think about which ones would accept her and how she would afford any of them.

BROWN V. THE BOARD OF EDUCATION OF TOPEKA

In 1896, in the case *Plessy v. Ferguson*, the U.S. Supreme Court ruled that private businesses in the United States (specifically railroads) could be racially segregated as long as the services provided were equal. This supported the idea that schools in the United States could be "separate but equal." In reality, U.S. schools were separate but seldom equal, and schools intended for African Americans received less government money. In 1954, with *Brown v. the Board of Education of Topeka*, all of this changed. In a lawsuit against the Topeka Board of Education, thirteen parents called for the integration of Topeka schools. Thurgood Marshall, a lawyer for the NAACP, argued the case before the Supreme Court, and on May 17, 1954, the court ruled unanimously that segregation was unconstitutional. This decision paved the way for integration and played a key role in the civil rights movement. Many schools resisted integration, however, and in some instances, it took more than a decade for integration to really begin.

Jordan's debate coach, Tom Freeman, suggested Boston University (BU). He reminded her that BU had been admitting women for decades, and some African-American women were already enrolled in the law school. Jordan thought about what it would be like to leave Texas and go to school in Massachusetts. She told no one in her family at first, but she applied and was accepted. Jordan was off to Boston!

MAKING ADJUSTMENTS

Once she got settled in Boston, Jordan realized just how unprepared she was. Her classmates had been more exposed to theater, literature, music, and other aspects of culture than she ever had. Many of them were also wealthy, and they could easily afford new clothes and cars. Jordan was lucky that her family chipped in to help her financially, but she had to watch every penny. When she had announced her wish to go to Boston University, her father had read through the fees and said,

This is more money than I have ever spent on anything or anyone. But if you want to go, we'll manage.

As Jordan started classes, she was in for another shock. She had always been a good student, but law school was much harder than anything she had experienced before. No longer could she just memorize facts; she had to prove to her professors that she could use logic and reason. She had to show how she figured out solutions to problems.

BOSTON UNIVERSITY

Boston University is a private institution that traces its beginnings to 1839, when a group of Methodist ministers established the Newbury Biblical Institute in Vermont. Eventually the school moved to Brookline, Massachusetts, and became the Boston Theological Institute. In 1869, the school moved again and became Boston University. A rarity at that time, every department of the university was open to people of all races and genders. The Boston University School of Law was founded in 1872. Today, Boston University has more than 30,000 students and is one of the largest private universities in the United States.

During her first year, Jordan was very lonely. She missed her family, her church, and her friends. But she got to know her roommate, LaConyea Butler, and she became friends with Issie Shelton, who was also from Houston. Jordan also found a friend in Louise Bailey, whose father was chairman of the Democratic National Committee (DNC). The DNC is one of the two main political groups in the United States (the other is the Republican National Committee, or RNC). Before long Jordan met more people through Bailey, and the loneliness began to subside.

Hoping desperately not to fail, Jordan struggled through her first semester. She didn't want to disappoint her family—or herself. She remembered,

" I didn't get much sleep during those years. I was lucky if I got three or four hours a night, because I had to stay up. I had to. "

That first year, Jordan spent a lonely Christmas in Boston because she couldn't afford to travel to Texas. And she worried about the grades that would be posted in January. Would she pass? Or would she have to go home to Houston as a failure?

MAKING PROGRESS

Jordan got a grade of 79 that first semester. She was far from the top of her class, but she had passed. Now she had to dig in and survive another semester. The rest of the year turned out to be easier. She joined a study group, which practiced talking out answers and discussing cases. At the end of her second semester, Jordan had a 78.4 average. She was ready for a summer visit to Houston, and her father made sure she had the money to get there.

The next year, Jordan returned to Boston with more energy and determination. She spent more time preparing for classes and better understood what was expected of her. She also made time to attend church at Marsh Chapel, where she

Edward Brooke III poses for a photo during his time in the U.S. Senate.

found the messages of the sermons comforting and encouraging.

During this time, a professor suggested that Jordan meet Edward Brooke III, a local attorney who went on to serve in the U.S. Senate. Brooke gave Jordan helpful advice about her law career. She appreciated the time he made for her.

TRAGEDY AND TRIUMPH

During Jordan's third year of law school, she suffered a great personal loss. Grandpa Patten had begun to drink heavily. One day he stumbled onto the railroad tracks and was struck by a train, which severed his legs. Jordan rushed to see him and arrived just in time. At the hospital she squeezed his hand, he looked up at her, and then he passed away. She had always wanted to make Patten proud, to make something of her life. Losing him was difficult, but she became more determined to do something special with her life.

EDWARD BROOKE III

Edward Brooke III (1919–) was born in Washington, D.C. He earned an undergraduate degree from Howard University and went on to graduate from Boston University Law School in 1948. In 1962, he was elected attorney general of Massachusetts. In 1966, when Brooke was elected to the U.S. Senate, he became the first African American to serve in the Senate since the 1800s, as well as the first African American elected to the Senate by popular vote. Though he was a member of the Republican Party, he often voted with the Democrats. Brooke coauthored the Fair Housing Act, which President Johnson signed into law in 1968, and he was the first Republican to call for President Nixon's resignation. In 2004, Brooke received the Presidential Medal of Freedom, the highest honor bestowed on American civilians.

In 1959, Jordan finished law school and enjoyed her family's visit to Boston to see her receive her diploma. It was a wonderful day for all of them. She then passed the Massachusetts bar exam and began to contemplate where she wanted to work. She thought about staying in Boston, but then she realized how much she missed home.

Jordan decided to return to Houston. She could use her law degree to help the people of her home state. She took the Texas bar exam and became just the third female African-American lawyer in Texas.

Entering
Politics

A FTER SPENDING HER LAW SCHOOL YEARS in Boston, Barbara Jordan was convinced that black and white Americans could live and work together. She had witnessed integration, and she had been a part of it. But racial equality was slow in coming to the South as well as other parts of the country. Schools remained segregated throughout most of Houston, and Jordan observed injustices throughout the city.

This was a time of great change in the United States. The civil rights movement was in full swing, and African Americans were finding ways to demand their rights. In 1955, in Montgomery, Alabama, an African-American woman named Rosa Parks had been arrested for refusing to give up her seat to a white man on a city bus. This act helped start the Montgomery Bus Boycott, which received national attention. Leaders such as Martin Luther King Jr. urged African Americans to stand up for their rights in peaceful ways.

WORKING IN HER COMMUNITY

Once Jordan decided to stay in Houston, she passed out business cards at church and set up her "office" on her parents' dining room table. Soon she was writing wills and helping people with other legal issues.

At this time, Houston was a vibrant, booming city, but many of its African Americans lived very close to the poverty

Martin Luther King Jr. (*center*) walks down an Atlanta street after participating in a civil rights protest.

MARTIN LUTHER KING JR.

Martin Luther King Jr. (1929–1968) was born in Atlanta, Georgia. As a minister and a leader in the civil rights movement, King led the Montgomery Bus Boycott in Alabama. He also helped found the Southern Christian Leadership Conference, an American civil rights organization. King urged his followers to stand up against racial discrimination, but he supported only peaceful means of protest. In 1963, King led the March on Washington, an enormous demonstration focused on racial issues. There he delivered his now-famous "I Have a Dream" speech. In 1964, King became the youngest recipient of the Nobel Peace Prize. King's life was cut short in 1968 when he was assassinated in Memphis, Tennessee.

Martin Luther King Jr. shakes hands with President Lyndon Johnson (*left*) after Johnson signs the Civil Rights Act of 1964.

line. About one-quarter of the city's African Americans made only about two thousand dollars a year. The vast majority were not business owners but instead had to work for other people. So it was important to them that Jordan be there, in their community, to help with any legal issues that they faced.

Jordan also decided to volunteer for John F. Kennedy's presidential campaign. She had learned about Kennedy in Boston and wanted to see him elected in 1960. His running mate was Lyndon Baines Johnson of Texas.

Jordan spent many hours sending out mailings and urging people to vote for Kennedy and Johnson. She also got to know some of the Democratic Party leaders in her state. Chris Dixie of the Harris County Democrats was especially impressed with Jordan.

At a meeting one night, a speaker had to cancel at the last minute. Jordan was asked to fill in. She surprised herself with the force and influence of her own voice. People listened to her and wanted to hear more about what she had to say. Before she knew it, leaders of the Democratic Party had scheduled her to speak more. She remembered,

"There was the novelty of my being a black woman lawyer, and graduating from a law school in Boston, and sounding different. That got attention."

Jordan enjoyed talking to people about Kennedy and Johnson, and she found herself enthralled by politics. Even after President Kennedy was elected, she continued to work on a local level by encouraging people to vote and to get involved in the political process.

JOHN F. KENNEDY

John F. Kennedy (1917–1963) was born into a political family in Brookline, Massachusetts. After serving as a U.S. representative from Massachusetts and then as a U.S. senator,
Kennedy earned the Democratic nomination for president in
1960. He defeated Republican candidate Richard Nixon and
became the youngest person (at age forty-three) elected to
the office. A gifted speaker, Kennedy is often remembered
for this famous line from his inauguration speech: "Ask not
what your country can do for you; ask what you can do for
your country." Kennedy led the way for the creation of the
Peace Corps, a program focused on helping people in devel-
oping countries, and he was a supporter of the civil rights
movement. On November 22, 1963, an assassin shot and
killed Kennedy while he was on a political trip in Texas.

John F. Kennedy (*upper center*) greets a crowd while campaigning for president in 1960.

BECOMING A CANDIDATE

After the 1960 presidential race, Jordan's law practice expanded. She opened a law office in the Fifth Ward, and her list of clients grew. Meanwhile, Chris Dixie was convinced that Jordan should run for political office. But could an African American woman be elected in Texas?

Dixie encouraged Jordan to run for the Texas state legislature, and before long she was ready to try. In 1962 she ran against Willis Whatley, a white man, and she knew she had to appeal to both black and white voters. She traveled the district and explained her ideas to voters. She supported increased funding for poorer colleges, and she planned to help the needy and the elderly.

When the votes were in, Jordan was very disappointed. She had lost. Although she had won over many African Americans, white voters were not convinced.

Two years later, Jordan tried again and faced the same candidate. Again she lost. But somehow, Jordan just knew she was destined for political office.

A TIME OF CHANGE

The 1960s were a decade of huge change, marked by race and civil rights issues. In addition to lingering racial segregation, some citizens still were denied the right to vote. Unfair poll taxes and difficult voting tests frightened African Americans away from voter registration offices.

In 1963, President John F. Kennedy, a supporter of civil rights, was assassinated, and Lyndon Johnson became president. Johnson made great progress while in office, and he signed several important

LYNDON B. JOHNSON

Lyndon B. Johnson (1908–1973) was born near Stonewall, Texas. He served five terms in the Texas legislature and later was elected a U.S senator. After gaining much popularity in the Senate, Johnson served as vice president under John F. Kennedy. When Kennedy was assassinated in 1963, Johnson became president of the United States. The following year, he ran for the office and was elected. While president, Johnson signed the Civil Rights Acts of 1964 and 1968, and he helped create a medical program called Medicaid. In 1968 Johnson chose not to run for president and left the Democratic Party deeply divided. He passed away in 1973 after suffering his third heart attack.

bills into law. One of them was the Civil Rights Act of 1964, which banned racial segregation in public places. Another was the Voting Rights Act of 1965, which restored and protected voting rights for everyone and ended the unfair poll taxes. There was hope, but there was still a lot of work to do.

MAKING A NAME FOR HERSELF

In 1965 Jordan was offered an incredible opportunity. Bill Elliott, a judge in Harris County, offered her a job as his assistant, and she leaped at the opportunity. Before this, African Americans had worked in courthouses only as custodians. Suddenly Jordan had an important position, and people were taking notice.

As Judge Elliott's assistant, Jordan was able to implement programs to help people get jobs and get off welfare. She also found ways for county offices to run more efficiently. Through this position, Jordan met many new people—both black and white—and became better known.

Traveling through Houston, Jordan saw that her state still needed to make some changes. Ten years after *Brown v. Board of Education of Topeka*, most white and black students still attended separate schools. The Supreme Court decision had said that schools should integrate "with all deliberate speed," but that had not happened. The NAACP challenged the school boards and took them to court, but progress was slow.

Jordan worked with Reverend William Lawson to cofound a group called People for Upgraded Schools in Houston (PUSH). The members organized a peaceful protest in which African Americans boycotted Houston schools for a day. The students joined civil rights leaders and marched in front of the school board headquarters.

This got the school board's attention, and members of the board met with members of PUSH. Further, the U.S. Department of Justice ordered that all schools in all grades be integrated by 1966. The work of Jordan and others had made a difference, and it had set an example for the nation.

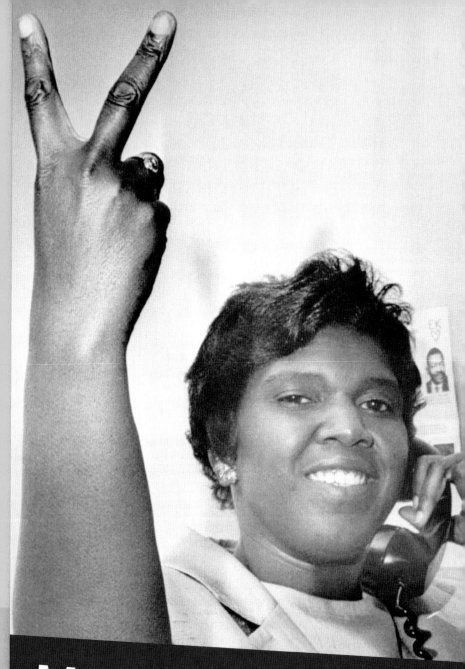

CHAPTER FOUR

Making History

I N 1963, ANOTHER SUPREME COURT RULING played an important part in Barbara Jordan's life. The case *Gray v. Sanders* led to the one-person, one-vote, law. This meant that each legislative district had to have the same number of people. Thus, throughout the 1960s, district boundaries had to be redrawn in various states. Suddenly, Senate District Eleven of Texas incorporated the Fifth Ward and some other areas that Jordan had carried in her previous campaigns. It was time for her to run for office once again.

ON THE CAMPAIGN TRAIL

Jordan announced that she would seek office in 1966, not for the state legislature but for the Texas State Senate. In the Democratic primary, she faced a tough opponent named Charles Whitfield. He tried to convince her not to run, but she was not swayed. She knew she had a good group of people backing her.

Before her campaign began, Jordan had to quit her courthouse job, since she couldn't work for the county while running for a state office. During this time her old high school friend and debate team member, Otis King, offered her a job that didn't conflict with her campaigning.

Barbara Jordan offers a victory sign after winning the Democratic nomination to the Texas State Senate in 1966.

Jordan made the rounds again. She met people and gave speeches. She sent out flyers that showed voters exactly how to cast their ballots. She won the support of the Harris County Democrats, and she earned the endorsement of the *Texas Observer* newspaper.

Election day was May 8, and when the votes were counted, history had been made. Barbara Jordan had received 64 percent of the vote! She had won the primary, and since there was no Republican to face her in the general election, she had won a seat in the Texas State Senate.

IN THE STATE SENATE

On January 10, 1967, Barbara Jordan stood in the Texas State Capitol and took the oath of office. She was the first African American since 1883—and the first African-American woman—ever to hold the position. This was a huge accomplishment, not just for Jordan but also for the nation. Newspapers all over the country told her story.

Once she took her seat in the senate, Jordan knew she needed to do a good job. She got to know the other senators, and she studied the rules of the senate. However, she was in a world dominated by white men. She had to find a way to be accepted among them.

Being on committees is an important way to get things done in any legislature. Jordan asked for appointments to two committees. Lieutenant Governor Preston Smith, who presided over the senate, gave Jordan both assignments—on the labor and management committee and on the state affairs committee—as well as several others. Soon Jordan was learning all the ins and outs of the senate.

When it came time to vote, Jordan was careful to study the

bills and to master their details. She supported a minimum wage law (even though it failed), and she opposed additional sales taxes. Jordan thought about how new laws would impact the people she represented.

On March 21, 1967, Jordan made history again. During long debates in the senate, Lieutenant Governor Smith would often excuse himself and let someone else preside over the senate for a short time. On that day, Smith gave that responsibility to Jordan, and she became the first African American elected official ever to preside over the Texas State Senate. At the end of her first session, Jordan's fellow senators elected her as outstanding freshman senator.

A BALANCING ACT

Barbara Jordan was driven to do a good job in the Texas State Senate, but she had a lot to juggle. Her salary was not very high, so she maintained her law practice in Houston. She found herself pulled in many directions as she tried to work with her fellow representatives, to please her constituents, and to find time for herself. She was lucky to be a part of a group of white women friends in Houston. The group included Betty Whitaker, a social worker; Anne Appenzellar, director of the Austin YWCA; and Nancy Earl, an educational psychologist who worked for the University of Texas. Jordan, who enjoyed playing the guitar, would get together with her friends to sing, to go camping, and just to spend time together. Jordan was relieved that no one in this group wanted political favors from her. Many of these women remained lifelong friends.

IMPORTANT ISSUES

In the 1960s Americans were fighting several forms of discrimination. For example, unfair housing practices often affected African Americans. In 1967 Jordan received a telegram asking her to join President Lyndon Johnson and other leaders to discuss a fair housing law. She was shocked. She had never been summoned to Washington before! Jordan was thrilled to go and meet with Roy Wilkins and

Barbara Jordan takes part in a meeting held in the Texas Cabinet Room in 1967.

THE CIVIL RIGHTS ACT OF 1968

Late in his presidency, Lyndon Johnson signed the Civil Rights Act of 1968 into law. Part of that law, which is also known as the Fair Housing Act, was a follow-up to the Civil Rights Act of 1964 and was intended to prevent discrimination in the nation's housing industry. For many years, African Americans had been treated differently from other people when they tried to rent or buy a home. The new law prohibited unfair practices in the sale, rental, and financing of housing based on a person's race, religion, color, or national origin. In 1974 lawmakers added gender to the list of protected groups, and in 1988 the law was expanded to prohibit discrimination based on disability or familial status.

other civil rights leaders. Their work eventually led to the Civil Rights Act of 1968.

During the meeting in Washington, President Johnson singled Jordan out. At one point he asked, "Barbara, what do you think?" Jordan was honored that the president wanted to hear her ideas. Soon President Johnson was consulting her on other issues as well. One day Jordan's mother was astonished to answer their home phone and to hear that the president was calling for her daughter.

In April 1968, Jordan joined the rest of the nation in mourning the death of Martin Luther King Jr., who was assassinated while in Memphis, Tennessee. She and other leaders were making progress on civil rights issues, but King's death seemed to set everyone back. A few months later, in June 1968, Robert Kennedy, John F. Kennedy's brother, was assassinated while campaigning for the Democratic nomination for president. It was a turbulent time for all Americans.

THE VIETNAM WAR

When Jordan served in the Texas State Senate, the Vietnam War (1959-1975) was still raging. This war was a conflict between North Vietnam and South Vietnam, but its outcome affected many nations. One of the main reasons for the war was to combat communism. Under a communist system, a nation's government owns all the property, and people rely on the government for everything. The United States became involved in the war in an attempt to prevent communism from spreading from North Vietnam to South Vietnam—and possibly to other parts of the world. During the second part of the twentieth cen-

An explosion erupts as U.S. troops patrol South Vietnam in 1966.

tury, the United States and the Union of Soviet Socialist Republics (USSR) were involved in the Cold War. This was an era of political conflict based on tensions between communism and both democracy and capitalism.

Many people in the United States did not support the Vietnam War. They could see no justification for sending U.S. troops to Vietnam. But a military draft began in 1970, and men eighteen and older were required to register—and possibly be enlisted— for service.

While Lyndon Johnson was president, the fighting in Vietnam escalated. Jordan was unsure of her own views about the war. She was very loyal to Johnson, however, so she backed his policies.

Throughout the United States, college students and other citizens protested both the war and the draft. During the conflict, more than 3 million U.S. soldiers served in Vietnam and more than 58,000 lost their lives. In 1975, the United States finally pulled out of the conflict, and South Vietnam fell to North Vietnam. By that time, the United States had spent approximately $111 billion on the war (an amount equal to nearly $700 billion today), and the government had accrued a huge debt.

GETTING THINGS DONE

Jordan was elected to a second term in the Texas State Senate in 1968. During the next four years, she worked to pass legislation that would help the people of her state. For example, she helped pass a law that set a minimum wage for most Texas workers. She worked on laws that made the workplace fair for everyone. She supported a bill that allowed injured workers to receive part of their pay (workers' compensation) even when they couldn't physically do their jobs. She also opposed a bill that placed taxes on food because she knew it would hurt the poorer people of her state. Jordan didn't win every fight, but she learned how to compromise and did her best with each issue.

NEW DISTRICTS

The 1970 census revealed that the population of Texas had grown. Since a state's number of representatives in the U.S. House of Representatives is based on population, Texas would receive one more seat in the House, effective with the 1972 election.

Former president Johnson strongly felt that Houston should get the new district, and he wanted Jordan to run for the seat. For Jordan, it seemed that everything pointed to a future bid for the U.S. House of Representatives. While she had done a fine job in Texas government, she could have even more influence as part of Congress.

CHAPTER FIVE

Representative Jordan

I N OCTOBER 1971, BARBARA JORDAN HOSTED a fund-raiser for her congressional campaign. Some 1,500 people came, and Jordan realized she had come a long way from the Fifth Ward. The room was filled with bankers, lawyers, and businesspeople of all backgrounds. Lyndon Johnson was in poor health after having suffered a heart attack, but he attended the event to offer his support. While addressing the crowd, he said,

> **Barbara Jordan proved to us that black is beautiful before we knew what that meant. . . . Those with hurting consciences because they have discriminated against blacks and women can vote for Barbara Jordan and feel good.**

But one person was not so enthusiastic. Curtis Graves had won a seat in the Texas House of Representatives when Jordan originally was elected to the Texas State Senate. Graves hoped to take Jordan's place. But now that the districts had been

President Lyndon Johnson and Barbara Jordan share a laugh at a fund-raiser in 1971.

redrawn, the district he had been counting on had changed suddenly. When district boundaries change, districts sometimes become dominated by voters of one race. Graves was angry with Jordan, and he announced that he would challenge her in the Democratic primary. He never really had a chance of winning, however. In May 1972, Jordan won the primary with 80 percent of the vote.

LEAVING THE SENATE

Once Jordan won the primary, it was clear she wouldn't be returning to the Texas State Senate. Her years there had been important to her, and in some ways she was sad to go. The following month, the legislature called a special session just for Jordan. Lieutenant Governor Ben Barnes made her president pro tempore of the senate. Then Governor Smith and Lieutenant Governor Barnes left the state on government business for the day. What did that mean? On June 10, 1972, Barbara Jordan was the governor of Texas for a day!

Thousands of people traveled to Austin to help Jordan celebrate. Friends and family came, as did the TSU choir and the Phillis Wheatley High School band. Many businesses in the Fifth Ward closed to mark the occasion. Jordan rented a hotel suite for her close friends and family, and she enjoyed the historic event. Never before had an African-American woman been governor of Texas—if only temporarily.

The day was not a completely joyful one, however. Right after the reception for Jordan, her father, Benjamin, collapsed and was taken to the hospital. Jordan didn't want to dampen everyone's spirits, so she stayed to listen the choir and the band and to take part in the meal. But soon she slipped out to the hospital to see her father. Benjamin had suffered a stroke, and he fell into a coma later that night. He died and was buried in Houston.

Barbara Jordan serves as the governor of Texas for one day, on June 10. 1972. It was a temporary position, but a great honor for her.

At this time, Jordan's feelings for her father were complicated. After returning from Boston, she had discovered that Benjamin had been involved with a woman other than her mother. This had hurt Jordan, and she had lost some respect for him. Further, she had grown tired of his need to control the family. However, Jordan still was grateful for all the encouragement and support that her father had given her over the years.

GOING TO WASHINGTON

The following fall, Jordan faced Republican Paul Merritt in the general congressional election, but he was not a serious contender. She won the race by a landslide and was officially elected to the U.S. House of Representatives. Newspapers across the nation covered the story and featured her photograph.

In January 1973, Jordan took the oath of office for her new position. She became the first African-American woman from the South, and the first female Texan, to serve in Congress. She had a big job ahead of her, and she wanted to learn how to be effective in Washington. Jordan represented about 500,000 people in Texas, and she wanted to do all that she could for them. Her goals were to continue to fight discrimination, to create a better society for the poor and the needy, and to enable all citizens to be part of the political process.

The Texas State Senate has just thirty-one senators, so it didn't take long for Jordan to get to know everyone while she was there. But in Congress, she was one of 435 representatives. This was a huge change, and Jordan knew she would have to find ways to be accepted and to make a difference.

As with the Texas legislature, Jordan knew that she had to join

In 1973, several female members of the U.S. House of Representatives meet together. From left to right: Martha Griffiths, Shirley Chisholm, Elizabeth Holtzman, Barbara Jordan, Yvonne Braithwaite Burke, and Bella Abzug.

a committee to get things done. The Congressional Black Caucus wanted her to serve on the House Armed Services Committee, but she wasn't sure if that was the best place for her. She thought her background in law would be useful on the House Judiciary Committee. Since these were major committees, she couldn't sit on both, so she asked former president Johnson for his advice.

Johnson advised Jordan to choose the House Judiciary Committee. He said that if she ever wanted to be a federal judge, experience on that committee would pave the way. He also said that the House Armed Services Committee might be too controversial—not the best

CONGRESSIONAL BLACK CAUCUS

The Congressional Black Caucus was founded in 1969, when the number of African-American members of Congress was increasing. Among its goals are improving social programs for African Americans and ensuring that African Americans have a voice in U.S. government. The group's founders include Shirley Chisholm of New York, Louis Stokes of Ohio, John Conyers of Michigan, and William L. Clay of Missouri. Although the caucus is open to all political parties, most members are Democrats. The caucus has honorary members who are white, Jewish, and Hispanic, but official members are all African American.

choice for a young member of Congress. Jordan took Johnson's advice and asked to be placed on the Judiciary Committee.

GETTING TO KNOW CONGRESS

Being a woman in Congress was a challenge for Jordan because there were so few. For instance, she found out that women had never been invited to the Texas Democratic Delegation Luncheon. Why was that? Were women just not interested in this group, or was the group not receptive to women? Jordan set out to change this kind of exclusion. She made it clear that she wanted to be part of the group, and the delegation accepted her and even elected her as its secretary.

Jordan also became part of the Congressional Black Caucus and joined its two other women: Shirley Chisholm of New York and Yvonne Brathwaite Burke of California. Andrew Young, also a member of the caucus, was the other southern African American who had a seat in Congress at this time.

Some members of the caucus were unsure what to think about Barbara Jordan. First, she declined to join the House committee that the group had recommended. Second, she chose not to sit with them in Congress. Instead, she liked to sit in the center, where she was more visible and accessible. And third, she didn't always vote the way the caucus wanted her to. Her main concern was to support bills that she believed in—not just those that the caucus supported.

LOSING A FRIEND

Jordan had barely taken office when she received sad news. Her friend and supporter, Lyndon Johnson, had passed away. After suffering from heart disease for many years, he died of a heart attack on

SHIRLEY CHISHOLM

Shirley Chisholm (1924–2005) was born in Brooklyn, New York, and was educated as a teacher. She became involved in community affairs, entered politics, and was elected to the New York State Assembly. Four years later, in 1968, when she was elected to the U.S. House of Representatives, she became the first African-American woman elected to Congress. In 1972 she ran as a Democratic candidate for president of the United States—the first woman ever to do so. During her time in Congress, Chisholm cofounded the Congressional Black Caucus, fought for minimum wage laws, supported heath care and education, and served on the House Committee on Education and Labor. In 1993 Chisholm was inducted into the National Women's Hall of Fame.

January 22, 1973. Jordan appreciated all that Johnson had done for her and for the people of the nation. She said,

> **Old men straightened their stooped backs because Lyndon Johnson lived; little children dared look forward to intellectual achievement because he lived; black Americans became excited about a future of opportunity, hope, justice, and dignity.**

In 1971 Johnson had published his memoirs, and he had opened the Lyndon Baines Johnson Library and Museum near the University of Texas at Austin. The library was a symbol of pride in the progress that occurred during his administration. Among other records, all of Johnson's civil rights papers are housed there. When Jordan visited Johnson at the library once, he told her that signing the Civil Rights Act of 1964 was his greatest accomplishment. She agreed.

WORKING HARD

In the 1970s the women's rights movement had gained momentum. Women in the United States were no longer content to be wives and mothers only. They wanted careers outside the home, and they wanted to branch out beyond traditionally female jobs as teachers, nurses, and administrative assistants.

EQUAL RIGHTS AMENDMENT

The Equal Rights Amendment (ERA) has a long history. In 1920 the Nineteenth Amendment to the U.S. Constitution granted women the right to vote. Alice Paul, a women's suffrage leader, introduced the Equal Rights Amendment just three years later, in 1923. Since then lawmakers have introduced the amendment in Congress numerous times, but it has never been ratified fully. In the 1970s some people criticized the ERA because they felt it blurred the lines between the genders. Even though the amendment never became official, many of its provisions have made their way into other laws. However, many people still argue that women earn less money than men who perform the same jobs.

By becoming a lawyer and then a politician, Jordan was living the life of a feminist, but she seldom labeled herself that way. She supported the Equal Rights Amendment, and she rejected any law that discriminated against women.

The issue of feminism hit home for Jordan after her father's death. Her mother, who was sixty-six at the time, was ineligible for Social Security benefits of her own because she had never worked outside the home. This seemed unfair to Jordan, and she discovered that many elderly women in her district had the same problem. She and Martha Griffiths of Michigan cosponsored a bill to provide Social Security benefits to homemakers. The bill was not successful, but laws passed since then provide more benefits to homemakers after the death of their spouses.

WOMEN'S RIGHTS

Jordan quickly found that being a congresswoman was a demanding job. She often worked twelve hours a day and then put in more time at home. She wanted to be as prepared as possible for every situation, and she wanted to understand fully every bill before her. She enlisted her staff to research issues and to brief her on every detail. Fellow representatives were impressed with Jordan's level of preparation.

For the first time in her life, Jordan was financially comfortable. She no longer had to save every dollar, and she was able to close her law practice while she was in Congress. Having money was a huge relief to her, and in time she even grew less worried about spending some of it.

Jordan was making a name for herself in Congress, and she was finding ways to get things done. For example, she managed to amend a crime control bill so that more African-American police officers

Women march for equal rights in New York City in August 1970. Barbara Jordan supported the rights of women and all citizens.

might be hired. Jordan supported bills that would help the oil executives of her state. Some people criticized her support of these big corporations, but Jordan knew that the oil industry was important to everyday people in Texas as well. But all these successes and compromises were just the beginning. In the years to come, events in the United States would challenge Jordan in remarkable ways.

CHAPTER SIX

The National Spotlight

I N 1972, THE UNITED STATES WAS THRUST into a time of uncertainty and disappointment. This new era involved burglary, spying, and secret informants. No one was sure how the drama would play out.

Republican Richard M. Nixon had been elected president of the United States in 1968, and he was reelected in 1972. Nixon's priorities were in stark contrast to those of the Democrats. Jordan and other members of Congress were upset when he canceled certain social programs. They also were angry that he sometimes didn't spend money in the ways Congress intended it to be spent. Jordan worried that the people of Texas were hurting because of Nixon's actions. But things were about to get worse.

THE WATERGATE SCANDAL

In June 1972, about five months before Nixon's reelection, five men were arrested for breaking into the Democratic National Committee headquarters in the Watergate office building. One of the arrested men served on Nixon's reelection committee. It appeared that the men had been spying on the Democrats in hopes of ensuring Nixon's victory.

As authorities investigated the crimes of these men, it became clear that more people had been involved. Nixon staffers, along

Barbara Jordan chats with George McGovern, the Democratic candidate for president in 1972. McGovern lost the election to Richard Nixon.

with other men connected to the president, had illegally tapped the phones and offices of the Democrats and had broken into their head-quarters. As the investigation continued into 1973, it became appar-ent that President Nixon had known about these crimes and had tried desperately to cover them up.

The situation called into question President Nixon's integrity, and Americans weren't sure what to believe. The situation changed when it became known that President Nixon had taped all of his con-versations in the Oval Office. The Supreme Court ordered him to hand the tapes over to the investigators. At first Nixon refused to supply the tapes. Then he offered partial transcripts. But eventually he was forced to release all of the tapes, whose contents were very damaging to Nixon. They proved that he had had complete knowledge of the Watergate crimes and had tried to keep that a secret.

JUDGING NIXON

As the details of Watergate unfolded, some of President Nixon's key advisers were forced to resign. Then, in 1973, Vice President Spiro Agnew also resigned because he was under investigation for tax eva-sion. Gerald Ford, a U.S. representative from Michigan, replaced Agnew as vice president.

Through all the debate about Watergate, Barbara Jordan was not sure whether President Nixon should be impeached. Impeachment is a proceeding in which an official is charged with misconduct but is not necessarily removed from office. According to the Constitution, a president can be impeached for "treason, bribery, or other high crimes and misdemeanors." Did Nixon's actions fall into any of these categories? After Jordan learned about the tapes, she began to think that maybe Nixon did qualify for impeachment.

In February 1974, Congress asked the House Judiciary Committee to investigate the situation and to determine whether Nixon should be impeached. Jordan felt uncomfortable discussing the president's behavior, but she knew it was part of her job. The U.S. government has three branches of government for a very important reason: to prevent any one branch from growing too powerful. In this case the Supreme Court (part of the judicial branch) and the House of Representatives (part of the legislative branch) were both checking up on the president (head of the executive branch).

As the House Judiciary Committee conducted closed-door hearings about President Nixon, Jordan listened carefully to all the evidence. She didn't want to make a quick judgment about Nixon's guilt or innocence. She was careful not to talk to reporters about the hearings, and she didn't discuss the matter with her staff. Outside the hearings, she researched the Constitution and learned all that she could about impeachment.

In late July 1974, the committee decided it was time to open up their hearings to the public. Their discussions would now be televised, and each of the thirty-eight members of the committee would be allowed to speak. Jordan worried that the representatives would take the opportunity to grandstand—to attract attention to themselves with their speeches without directly dealing with the issue at hand. But the other committee members believed it was important to express their ideas directly to the American people.

SPEAKING TO A NATION

Jordan was scheduled to speak in the Watergate hearings on the evening of July 25, but by that afternoon, she still didn't know what she was going to say. She had thoughts in her head, but she had written

CONSIDERING WATERGATE

The Watergate scandal weighed heavily on Barbara Jordan's mind. She may not have agreed with many of President Nixon's policies, but she respected the office he held. However, she knew that the Watergate issue was tearing the country apart. In May 1974, she was asked to deliver the commencement address at Howard University in Washington, D.C.

Current events were an important part of Jordan's speech that day. She told the graduates:

> If one thing is clear about the erosion of civil liberties, it is that there is no clear line between freedom and repression. Freedom is the fluid, intangible condition of our society. It thrives in some periods, and it is beset in other periods. The events of the past few years and even the past few days have convinced us that it is possible for this country to stand on the edge of repression and tyranny and never know it. If the faith in the future is to be restored, if that which is good about the history of this country is to be regained, you must restore it; you must regain it.

nothing down. At around 6 p.m. she began to work on a draft, and she asked her secretary to stay to type it up for her. Later, at around 8:30 p.m., she walked into the committee room and prepared to speak to the nation. She began at 9 p.m.

> **My faith in the Constitution is whole, it is complete, it is total, and I am not going to sit here and be an idle spectator to the diminution, the subversion, the destruction of the Constitution.**

Barbara Jordan speaks about the issue of Nixon's impeachment on July 25, 1974.

Jordan talked about how President Nixon had abused his power. She listed his crimes and assured the people that her committee had the best interests of the nation in mind. And she told them that James Madison had explained at the Constitutional Convention in 1787, "A President is impeachable if he attempts to subvert the Constitution." With that in mind, she reminded her audience that Nixon had told his staff to lie to protect him from his own mistakes.

Jordan explained,

> **We know the nature of impeachment. We have been talking about it a while now. . . . If the impeachment provision will not reach the offenses here, then perhaps that eighteenth-century Constitution should be abandoned to a twentieth-century paper shredder.**

When Jordan finished speaking, the room was quiet. It was as if no one knew how to react to her words. Her argument had convinced a nation that their president had disregarded the very document that formed the federal government. Jordan's confident voice had made it clear what needed to happen next.

Within the next week, the U.S. House of Representatives voted to impeach President Nixon. The same vote by the U.S. Senate seemed likely. Before that could happen, President Nixon took matters into his own hands. On August 9, 1974, he announced his resignation as president of the United States, thus becoming the only president ever to do so.

RICHARD M. NIXON

Richard M. Nixon (1913–1994) was born in Yorba Linda, California. He received a degree from Duke University Law School in 1937. In 1946 he was elected to the U.S. House of Representatives, and four years later he was elected to the U.S. Senate. Nixon served as vice president under President Dwight Eisenhower from 1953 to 1961. In 1960 he ran for the presidency but was defeated by John F. Kennedy in a close race. In 1968 he ran for the presidency again and defeated Democratic nominee Hubert Humphrey. Four years later, he was reelected to the office. Nixon is remembered for helping end the Vietnam War and opening up U.S. relations with China. But he is probably most remembered for the Watergate scandal, which led to the end of his presidency. To date, Nixon is the only U.S. president to resign from office. In 1994 he suffered a stroke at his home in California and passed away. Nixon remains the only American to have been elected twice to both the vice presidency and the presidency.

President Richard Nixon is photographed in the Oval Office on February 2, 1974.

NEW CHALLENGES

After the Watergate hearings, Jordan was suddenly well known. Americans praised her intelligence and eloquence, and people from organizations throughout the nation asked her to speak. Jordan was careful to make speeches only about issues that were really important to her.

In the meantime, an important anniversary was approaching. The Voting Rights Act of 1965 was due for an extension in 1975. Beyond extending the law, Jordan wanted to change it to include Hispanics in Texas. The original law included just the states of the Deep South: Alabama, Georgia, Louisiana, Mississippi, South Carolina, Virginia, and North Carolina. Jordan was worried that Gerald Ford, who had become president when Nixon resigned, would not support the law. She had opposed Ford's earlier appointment as vice president because of his weak record on civil rights.

Jordan had to call in a number of favors and do a fair amount of politicking, but she managed to get the extension passed in the House. Then, with the help of Senators Robert Byrd and Mike Mansfield, the bill passed in the Senate as well. Support of the bill was so strong that President Ford had no choice but to sign it into law. His veto would have been overruled. This was a huge victory for Jordan and for voters everywhere.

FACING HEALTH ISSUES

Since 1973, Jordan had not been feeling well. She was hiding a medical secret: she'd been experiencing numbness and tingling in her hands and feet. These symptoms led to tests, and the test results led doctors to believe that she had multiple sclerosis. This disease

ROBERT BYRD

Robert Byrd (1917–2010) was born Cornelius Calvin Sale Jr. in North Wilkesboro, North Carolina. He was just a year old when his mother died, and he was sent to live with his aunt and uncle, who renamed him Robert Carlyle Byrd. He grew up in the coal-mining region of West Virginia. In 1952 Byrd was elected to the U.S. House of Representatives. He served until 1959, when he became a U.S. senator. He then went on to become the longest-serving member of the U.S. Congress until his death in 2010. Early in his career, Byrd was a member of the Ku Klux Klan, a white supremacist group that terrorized African Americans and opposed integration. He also opposed the Civil Rights Act of 1964 because he believed the law violated states' rights. Over the years his views changed, however, and he came to support the belief that all U.S. citizens deserve the same rights under the law. Today, he is remembered as a dedicated and respected public servant.

affects the nervous system and can cause severe disability. Jordan didn't want the pain to get in her way, and she hoped to hide the truth from the public. She kept the information from her family, and her staff was sworn to secrecy.

Jordan knew she was overweight, and the stress of her job was not helping her condition either. So she tried to lose weight, took the medication prescribed to her, and tried to control the disease that had struck her. As 1976 began, Jordan had lost weight but her feet still bothered her. She sometimes had trouble walking and using stairs.

CONTROVERSY AND CRITICISM

Throughout her career, Jordan always tried to stick to her beliefs no matter who tried to sway her. But sometimes this was easier said than done. Politics so often involves deals made with favors and compromises. It seems to be the way of Washington.

One example of this reality occurred in the case of John Connally. Jordan did not like Connally when he was governor of Texas. He was not a civil rights advocate, and he had opposed equal access to public facilities for African Americans. Further, he had angered Jordan with some of his remarks after Martin Luther King Jr. was killed. Jordan found herself in a difficult position, however.

Connally was being accused of bribery, and Robert Strauss of the Democratic National Party asked Jordan to testify as a character witness. First she said no, but Strauss pressed her. Then she realized that although she disliked Connally, she didn't think he had committed the bribery crimes. She agreed to testify as a favor to Strauss.

This decision made many people angry. They felt that Jordan had compromised her beliefs in the name of politics. This criticism began to bother Jordan, because she always had tried to be fair and impartial. She was also becoming discouraged because President Ford was vetoing more and more bills that she supported. Her job began to feel increasingly difficult.

LOOKING TO THE FUTURE

Around this time, Jordan's friend Nancy Earl was planning to build a home in Austin. She and Jordan had been longtime companions, and suddenly a quieter life seemed appealing. Jordan suggested that they build the house together, so she would have a place to go to escape reporters and other demands. One day, she could even retire there. In 1976 the construction of the house began, and the next chapter of Jordan's life seemed to be under way.

CHAPTER SEVEN

Jordan's Legacy

I N 1976 JIMMY CARTER WAS THE LIKELY Democratic candidate who would face incumbent Gerald Ford in the presidential race. It was an incredible honor when Barbara Jordan's party asked her to be the keynote speaker at the Democratic National Convention that year. Jordan was pleased to accept the invitation; she just hoped her feet would get her to the podium.

In the meantime, some people thought Carter might consider Jordan as his running mate. Though one poll suggested the Jordan was one of the twenty most trusted people in the nation, Jordan found it unlikely that an African-American woman would be nominated for vice president. Nevertheless, Jordan helped campaign for Carter since she believed he was a superior candidate to Ford.

THE KEYNOTE SPEECH

On July 12, 1976, Jordan delivered a history-making speech at the Democratic National Convention. It was titled "Who Then Will Speak for the Common Good?" Here are some highlights of that speech, much of which could be delivered today with equal relevance:

Barbara Jordan and Jimmy Carter wave to the crowd at the Democratic National Convention in 1976.

Who Then Will Speak
for the Common Good?

Now—Now that I have this grand distinction, what in the world am I supposed to say? I could easily spend this time praising the accomplishments of this party and attacking the Republicans—but I don't choose to do that. I could list the many problems which Americans have. I could list the problems which cause people to feel cynical, angry, frustrated: problems which include lack of integrity in government; the feeling that the individual no longer counts; the reality of material and spiritual poverty; the feeling that the grand American experiment is failing or has failed. I could recite these problems, and then I could sit down and offer no solutions. But I don't choose to do that either. The citizens of America expect more. They deserve and they want more than a recital of problems.

We are a people in a quandary about the present. We are a people in search of our future. We are a people in search of a national community. We are a people trying not only to solve the problems of the present, unemployment, inflation, but we are attempting on a larger scale to fulfill the promise of America. We are attempting to fulfill our national purpose, to create and sustain a society in which all of us are equal.

And now—now we must look to the future. Let us heed the voice of the people and recognize their common sense. If we do not, we not only blaspheme our political heritage, we ignore the common ties that bind all Americans. Many fear the future. Many are distrustful of their leaders, and believe that their voices are never heard. Many seek only to satisfy their private work—wants; to satisfy their private interests. But this is the great danger America faces—that we will cease to be one nation and become instead a collection of interest groups: city against suburb, region against region, individual against individual; each seeking to satisfy private wants. If that happens, who then will speak for America? Who then will speak for the common good?

A nation is formed by the willingness of each of us to share in the responsibility for upholding the common good. A government is invigorated when each one of us is willing to participate in shaping the future of this nation. In this election year, we must define the "common good" and begin again to shape a common future. Let each person do his or her part. If one citizen is unwilling to participate, all of us are going to suffer. For the American idea, though it is shared by all of us, is realized in each one of us.

And now, what are those of us who are elected public officials supposed to do? We call ourselves "public servants," but I'll tell you this: We as public servants must set an example for the rest of the nation. It is hypocritical for the public official to admonish and exhort the people to uphold the common good if we are derelict in upholding the common good. More is required—More is required of public officials than slogans and handshakes and press releases. More is required. We must hold ourselves strictly accountable. We must provide the people with a vision of the future.

If we promise as public officials, we must deliver. If—If we as public officials propose, we must produce. If we say to the American people, "It is time for you to be sacrificial"—sacrifice. If the public official says that, we [public officials] must be the first to give. We must be. And again, if we make mistakes, we must be willing to admit them. We have to do that. What we have to do is strike a balance between the idea that government should do everything and the idea, the belief, that government ought to do nothing. Strike a balance.

Let there be no illusions about the difficulty of forming this kind of a national community. It's tough, difficult, not easy. But a spirit of harmony will survive in America only if each of us remembers that we share a common destiny; if each of us remembers, when self-interest and bitterness seem to prevail, that we share a common destiny.

I have confidence that we can form this kind of national community.

REMAINING DAYS IN CONGRESS

Jordan easily won reelection to Congress in 1976, and many people speculated that President Carter would offer her a position in his cabinet. She hoped to become attorney general, a role in which she could strengthen civil rights, but the president promised to give the position to someone else.

Jordan was disappointed in the president's decision, and she began to become disappointed in Congress, too. The constant struggle to get bills passed was starting to weigh on her. And her health problems were becoming harder to hide.

The following year, in June 1977, Harvard University asked Jordan to deliver its commencement address and awarded her an honorary degree. She marveled at the irony: some twenty-five years earlier, she had been afraid to even apply to Harvard, and now that school was honoring her.

A few months later, in December 1977, Jordan announced that she would not seek another term in Congress. It was time to move on, and she knew there were other ways to make a difference in the nation.

PUBLIC AND PRIVATE LIFE

In 1979 Jordan became a professor at the University of Texas at Austin. She taught public policy courses in the Lyndon Baines Johnson School of Public Affairs. Jordan was very popular with her students, and she enjoyed spending time with them. She also attended Lady Longhorns basketball games whenever she could.

Jordan's health began to decline, and soon she was walking with a cane. Then she had to use a wheelchair. She found it difficult to get in and out of cars, but her students helped her, and she continued to teach throughout the rest of her life.

For several years Jordan stayed out of the public eye, but in 1984 she made appearances for candidates such as Senator Bill Bradley of New Jersey. Then, in 1987, she testified against Robert Bork, Ronald Reagan's choice for Supreme Court justice. Her arguments helped block Bork's appointment. The next year, she made a number of appearances on television, and she campaigned for the Democratic presidential candidate, Michael Dukakis. She gave the vice presidential nominating speech for Dukakis's running mate, Lloyd Bentsen of Texas, at the Democratic National Convention.

That summer, Jordan had a medical setback when she suffered cardiac arrest while swimming in her pool. Nancy Earl found Jordan's motionless body in the water and immediately thought the worst. But Jordan was rushed to the hospital and survived. However, the incident led to public disclosure of her multiple sclerosis.

FINAL YEARS

In 1991 Jordan began serving as ethics adviser to Texas governor Ann Richards. The following year, Jordan supported Bill Clinton for president of the United States, and she gave the keynote address at the convention that summer. Her health worsened, but that didn't keep her from attending his inauguration in January 1993. Jordan accepted Clinton's appointment as chair of the U.S. Commission on Immigration Reform.

President Clinton once stated that he would have liked to appoint Jordan to the Supreme Court, but by the time he could, her health prevented her from taking such a position. In 1994 Clinton presented Jordan with the Presidential Medal of Freedom, the highest honor a U.S. civilian can receive.

Also in 1994, Jordan found out that she had leukemia, an often

Barbara Jordan, her health failing, gives the keynote speech at the
Democratic National Convention on July 13, 1992.

fatal type of cancer. By winter 1995, she was growing weaker, and there was little hope for improvement. In January 1996, Jordan was getting ready for a new semester when she started having trouble breathing. She was rushed to the hospital and diagnosed with pneumonia, a complication associated with leukemia. On January 17, 1996, Jordan passed away. She was just shy of her sixtieth birthday.

REMEMBERING BARBARA

On January 20, 1996, hundreds of people gathered at Good Hope Baptist Church to pay their last respects to a remarkable woman. During the two-hour service, a number of people shared their memories of Jordan. Actress Cicely Tyson said,

> If I were sitting on a porch across from God, I would thank him for sending you to us.

Other speakers included Tom Freeman, Jordan's TSU debate coach, and Ann Richards, former governor of Texas. President Bill Clinton told the audience how nervous he had been the previous year when he was preparing to give a speech on race and the Constitution at the University of Texas and learned that Jordan would be present. Clinton said,

I think it was the nearest experience on this earth to the pastor giving a sermon with God in the audience.

Jordan's remains were taken to the Texas State Cemetery in Austin, and she was the first African American woman to be buried there. All of her papers and records are kept at the Barbara Jordan Archives at Texas Southern University.

In her famous speech during the Watergate hearings in July 1974, Barbara Jordan made an observation that sums up her life, as well as the progress of civil rights during her lifetime:

 Earlier today, we heard the beginning of the Preamble to the Constitution of the United States, 'We, the People.' It is a very eloquent beginning. But when that document was completed on the seventeenth of September 1787, I was not included in that 'We, the People.' I felt somehow for many years that George Washington and Alexander Hamilton just left me out by mistake. But through the process of amendment, interpretation, and court decision, I have finally been included in 'We, the People.'

AnN RICHARDS

Ann Richards (1933–2006) was born Dorothy Ann Willis in Lakeview, Texas, and grew up in Waco. She married David Richards, her high school sweetheart, and went to Baylor University on a debate scholarship. She then received her teaching certificate from Texas University and taught government classes at a junior high school. While raising her children, Richards campaigned for a number of political candidates. She served in local government and, in 1976, was elected Texas state treasurer.

Richards gave a nominating speech at the 1984 Democratic National Convention and was a keynote speaker four years later. These speeches brought her national attention. In 1990 Richards was elected governor of Texas. During her term she helped reform the state prison system and worked to allow African Americans and women to serve in the Texas Rangers, a state law enforcement agency. A charismatic person, Richards is known for her feminist views and remains one of the best-known politicians from Texas.

A statue of Barbara Jordan by artist Bruce Wolfe is located at Austin–Bergstrom International Airport, in Austin, Texas. The Barbara Jordan Passenger Terminal is named in her honor.

Today, Barbara Jordan is remembered as a legislator who was not afraid to speak out. She addressed issues of race, civil rights, women's rights, and constitutional law. A community center in Houston was named in her honor, as were schools and streets throughout the country. Her death may have silenced her voice, but her beliefs and ideals endure well into the twenty-first century.

TIMELINE

1936 — Barbara Charline Jordan is born on February 21 in Houston, Texas

1952 — Wins National United Ushers Association Oratorical Contest; graduates from Phillis Wheatley High School

1956 — Graduates with honors from Texas Southern University

1959 — Graduates from Boston University Law School

1962 — Runs for the Texas House of Representatives and loses

1964 — Loses a second campaign for the Texas legislature

1966 — Is elected to the Texas State Senate and becomes the state's first African-American senator since 1883

1968 — Wins second term in the Texas State Senate

1972 — Serves as Texas governor for a day; is elected to the U.S. House of Representatives and is assigned to the House Judiciary Committee

1973 — Begins to suffer from multiple sclerosis

1974 — Gains national recognition with a televised speech during the Watergate hearings; is elected to a second term in Congress

1976	Delivers the keynote speech at the Democratic National Convention; wins third congressional term
1979	Retires from public life; becomes professor at University of Texas at Austin
1987	Testifies against confirmation of Robert H. Bork to the U.S. Supreme Court
1992	Delivers the keynote speech at the Democratic National Convention
1993	Is appointed by President Clinton to chair the U.S. Commission on Immigration Reform
1994	Receives the Presidential Medal of Freedom
1996	Dies on January 17 in Austin, Texas

SOURCE NOTES

Boxed quotes unless otherwise noted

INTRODUCTION

p. 5, par. 3–5, American Rhetoric: Top 100 Speeches, http://www.americanrhetoric.com/speeches/barbarajordan1976dnc.html.

CHAPTER 1

p. 7, Mendelsohn, James. *Barbara Jordan: Getting Things Done* (Brookfield, CT: Twenty-First Century Books, 2000), p. 46.

p. 9, Crawford, Ann Fears. *Barbara Jordan: Breaking Barriers* (Houston: Halcyon Press, 2003), p. 7.

p. 13, Rogers, Mary Beth. *Barbara Jordan: American Hero* (New York: Bantam, 1998), pp. 3–4.

CHAPTER 2

p. 22, Jordan, Barbara, and Shelby Hearn. *Barbara Jordan: A Self-Portrait* (New York: Doubleday, 1979), p. 83.

p. 24, Crawford, *Barbara Jordan: American Hero*, p. 25.

CHAPTER 3

p. 31, Crawford, *Barbara Jordan: American Hero*, p. 31.

CHAPTER 5

p. 47, Jordan and Hearn, *Barbara Jordan: A Self-Portrait*, p. 159.

p. 55, Mendelsohn, *Barbara Jordan: Getting Things Done*, p. 140.

CHAPTER 6

p. 64, par. 3, Sherman, Max, editor. *Barbara Jordan: Speaking the Truth With Eloquent Thunder* (Austin: University of Texas Press, 2007), p. 18.

p. 65, Ibid., p. 27.

p. 66, Ibid., p. 28.

CHAPTER 7

pp. 74–77, American Rhetoric: Top 100 Speeches.

p. 81, Verhovek, Sam Howe, "At Funeral, Praise for Barbara Jordan," www.nytimes.com/1996/01/21/us/at-funeral-praise-for-barbara-jordan.html.

p. 82, top, Ibid.

p. 82, bottom, Sherman, *Barbara Jordan: Speaking the Truth With Eloquent Thunder*, p. 27.

FURTHER INFORMATION

BOOKS

Brill, Marlene Targ. *Multiple Sclerosis.* New York: Marshall Cavendish, 2008.

Kallen, Stuart A. *Women of the Civil Rights Movement.* San Diego: Lucent Books, 2005.

McConnell, William S. *Watergate.* New York: Greenhaven Press, 2005.

WEBSITES

American Rhetoric: Top 100 Speeches
Barbara Charline Jordan: 1976 Democratic National Convention
Keynote Address
Visit this site for a full text of Jordan's famous speech, as well as
an audio excerpt.
www.americanrhetoric.com/speeches/barbarajordan1976dnc.
html

Black Americans in Congress: Barbara Jordan
Find out more about Jordan's life and accomplishments.
http://baic.house.gov/member-profiles/profile.html?intID=67

BIBLIOGRAPHY

"Black Americans in Congress: Barbara Jordan" http://baic.house.gov/member-profiles/profile.html?intID=67

Clines, Francis X. "Barbara Jordan Dies at 59; Her Voice Stirred a Nation," *New York Times*, January 18, 1996. www.nytimes.com/1996/01/18/us/barbara-jordan-dies-at-59-her-voice-stirred-the-nation.html?pagewanted=2

Crawford, Ann Fears. *Barbara Jordan: Breaking Barriers*. Houston: Halcyon Press, 2003.

Jordan, Barbara, and Shelby Hearn. *Barbara Jordan: A Self-Portrait*. New York: Doubleday, 1979.

Mendelsohn, James. *Barbara Jordan: Getting Things Done*. Brookfield, CT: Twenty-First Century Books, 2000.

Rogers, Mary Beth. *Barbara Jordan: American Hero*. New York: Bantam, 1998.

Scarborough, Megan. "A Voice That Could Not Be Stilled." www.utexas.edu/features/archive/2003/jordan.html

Sherman, Max, ed. *Barbara Jordan: Speaking the Truth With Eloquent Thunder*. Austin: University of Texas Press, 2007.

Verhovek, Sam Howe. "At Funeral, Praise for Barbara Jordan," *New York Times*, January 21, 1996. www.nytimes.com/1996/01/21/us/at-funeral-praise-for-barbara-jordan.html

INDEX

ABOUT THE AUTHOR

LUCIA RAATMA is the author of dozens of books for young readers. She enjoys writing about historic events and famous people, as well as safety, environmental issues, and character education. She lives in the Tampa Bay area with her husband and their two children.